STAGE FEAR

101 Techniques to overcome the Stage Fear

Dr.Y.Narasimha Raja

Copy Rights Certification @ 2021

Stage Fear – 101 Techniques to overcome the Stage Fear
Dr. Y. Narasimha Raja -All rights reserved

MRP: Rs.200/- (Indian Rupees)
Amazon ISBN: 9798528856353
Publisher: Dr.Y.Narasimha Raja
297, Raja Nivas, 11th Main, 11th Cross-, Narsipura Layout,
Vidyaranyapura, Bangalore -560097, Karnataka, India
www.ynraja.com Email: ynr.phd@gmail.com
Contact: (+91) 8073205840
First Published in English, June 2021
Author & Editor: Dr. Y. Narasimha Raja

Readers note

The author has kept his highest efforts in writing this book. He respects all the readers and their feelings. He believes that all the re**ISBN:** 9798528856353aders are positive attitude icons. This book is written in simple English and self explanatory mode for the purpose of readers empowerment.

He sees, the readers to be Swan bird,
Who can separate milk from a mixture of water?

If you find any errors in this book, kindly forgive and observe the goodness of this book.

Let us be a player in life, who runs for the goal
& not a referee who looks for the faults

Language is just a means of communication; author has seen many thought provoking incidents, which has made him to pen down this book to spread awareness among us. Please extend positive thoughts &awareness of this book in the society.

With you and for you

Dr.Y.Narasimha Raja

Ph.D., MBA, M.Sc. Psychology, M.Com, MTM

About Author

 Dr. Y. Narasimha Raja is an International Trainer, Psychologist, Author, Coach, Mentor, Motivational speaker, counsellor and subject matter expert in his domain. He holds PhD degree in Management studies and multiple degrees that includes Master Business Administration, Master of Science in Psychology, Master of Commerce and Master of Tourism Management.

He has more than 18 years of vast corporate experience in India & abroad. He has served various global corporate companies as Lead HR. He has a proven track of delivering responsibilities Professional merits

Professional Awards & certifications

- "Best HR Practitioner " certifications from Construction Industry Development Council (CIDC) during – Vishwakarma Awards for the year 2019 associated body of NITI Agog
  (Formerly called Planning Commission of India).

- In his tenure, he has received several certifications for his performance from his organization viz *Merit of HR Operational Excellence, Well-done, systems & process, Great Job, Extra mile and many more.*

- He is certified as "Indian Management Styles" from the *Bangalore University* for the year 2002"

Personal Awards & Certifications

- 2002 Best Citizen Award - Andhra Pradesh Police
- 2000 Represented India South Asian Youth camp
- 1999 Represented India South Asian Youth Camp
- 2001 Pre Republic Parade – NSS
- 2002 N.C.C –Army Wing – C Certificate

Book Publications:

1. Highly Effective Parenting Skills
2. Highly Effective Teaching Skills
3. The best & smart Teaching techniques
4. Happy Parenting Skills
5. Stage Fear – 101 Techniques to overcome the stage fear.

International Journal publications -"International Organization of Scientific Research (IOSR) Volume 20, Issue 3. Ver. X (March. 2018)"

1. Why Employees are not willing to serve complete notice period during resignation?
2. Transformational Delegation is the Effective tool for Organization Excellence

His lectures, articles, seminars have created a tremendous impact on people and shown them the path to achieve success. Apart from his corporate experience, currently he is serving as Assistant professor at Presidency University, Bangalore.

Acknowledgement

We must give stand-up salute to the real heroes of the Nation i.e. Solders and Formers.

It is my honour to thank to Shri. **Anoop Singh Rathore**. *He has served the Nation in various levels in Border Security Force (BSF), Special Protection Force (SPG) and other risy & adventures army operations. He*  *is one of the proud son of the Mother India; he is a fearless person, lion hearted and unstoppable person. His patriotism and his achievements are the best inspiration to everyone. With best of my knowledge, his glorious achievements are as follows,*

- ✓ *He led the Camel Contingent – BSF as Commander, in eve of Indian Republic Day Parade for the consecutive years 2002 & 2003. Twice he has received Sword of Honour.*
- ✓ *Three appreciation letters received from then Three Prime Ministers of India.*
- ✓ *During operation Vijay star (Kargil), his posting was at Chourbata Sector as an Independent company commander for the BSF. During this time, the temperature in this area was minus 35 to minus 40 degrees.*
- ✓ *From 2003 to till date delivering lectures on VVIP security at Gujarat Police Academy Karai Gandhinagar as visiting Faculty.*

- ✓ *47 times he has received appreciation certificates from the Director SPG*
- ✓ *7 times he has received appreciation letters from the Deputy Director SPG*
- ✓ *One appreciation certification from one of the MOS*
- ✓ *One appreciation certification from the Principal Secretory Sh.T N Seshan*
- ✓ *5 times he has received appreciation certification from the DG commandation role BSF*
- ✓ *8 times he has received appreciation certifications from the IG from the BSF*
- ✓ *One appreciation certification from A.G– Gujarat Police*
- ✓ *One appreciation certification form IG Gujarat Police*

He believes age is a just number, after his defence experience; currently he is leading Administration Department for M/s. Kalpataru Power Transmission Ltd, Gandhinagar, and Gujarat, India.

Learning sessions with the Author

My sincere thanks goes to all the readers and their family members. Having trust on me and this subject book.

I guarantee this book will drive help to bring trust & happiness in family. Reading the book is not enough and it should come in practicality.

I am selling this book for the nominal cost, my primary intention is not to earn monitory profit from this book instead I believe in benefitting the reader out of this book.

As value addition to the readers, I will be imparting learning sessions by modes of videos, email and Whatsapp with the readers. To avail this services readers are requested to get connect with the author.

For Training, consultation, seminars get connect
Email: ynr.phd@gmail.com
WhatsApp: +91-9686845718
www.ynraja.com

Dedication

This book is dedicated to
My beloved parents
Mr.Y.Subba Ramaiah & Mrs. Y.Rajeswari.

Never forget two people in life!

*The first person who was with you in
every pain -**Mother** and
Second the person who lost everything
just to make you win -**Father.***

Preface

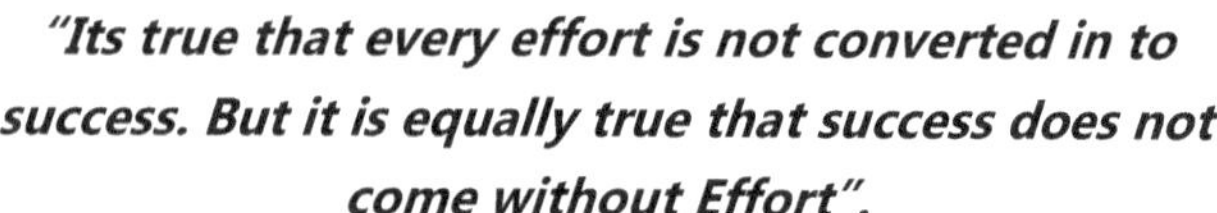

"Its true that every effort is not converted in to success. But it is equally true that success does not come without Effort".

This quote has inspired the author to keep his maximum efforts to write this book.

In this book How to overcome the stage fear and tips are emphasized. Reading and practicing these modernised qualities will help's the reader to overcome the stage fear and become highly effective public speaker.

It provides a broad range of information concisely and in an easy to read way. I assure, if these principles are applied in our practical life situation, we can defiantly view positive results with is fast span of time.

This book is written in simple English and self explanatory mode for the purpose of readers empowerment.

Never think I have nothing,,,,,
Never think I have everything,,,,,,
But, always think
I have something & I can achive anything

Contents

Chapter -1

About Stage Fear

"Once you become fearless,
Life becomes limitless"

It is the fear of Public speaking. "It is state of anxiety or fear or phobia or nervousness or fright or stress which happens when an individual is faced with the condition of performing in front of an audience (either directly or through a screen, e.g. in front of a camera). It affects all types of people who have to perform in front of an audience, even when they are not necessarily speaking." Performing in front of an unknown or first meeting audience can raise more nervousness than performing in front of familiar faces.

Stage fear is the inclination of worry and actual responses caused when speaking to others, extraordinarily to bigger gatherings.

Speech is the activity to convey the message to the audience and fear is the modern tendency of worry, nervousness, strain or concern that shows when feeling that negative things will occur and truly by expanded blood pressure, perspiring and shaking.

What are the other names / forms of Stage Fear?

1. Gloss phobia
2. Stage Fright
3. Speech Anxiety
4. Performance Anxiety

Where is the origin of Glossophobia?

The word glossophobia derives from the Greek glōssa, meaning tongue, and Phobos, fear or dread or anxiety.

Brief notes about Stage fear (Glossophobia)

In this consist manner, speech anxiety Glossophobia, or the fear of public speaking, is extremely common. Some experts estimate that as much as 77% of the population has some level of stress about Public Speaking Of course; many people can manage and control the fear. If your fear is significant, Glossophobia is a ***subdivision of Social phobia the fear of the social situation***.

Most people with glossophobia do not exhibit symptoms of other types of social phobia, such as panic about meeting new people or fear of performing tasks in front of others. Many

Glossophobia

people with glossophobia are able to dance or sing on stage, provided they do not have to talk. Nonetheless, stage fright is a relatively common experience in those with glossophobia.

Glossophobia may present a child desperately hoping she is not called on in class to answer a question. It may cause you to avoid situations where you may become the focus of attention.

Complications

The vast majority of careers involve some level of public speaking, from participating in meetings to giving presentations to clients. If your phobia is severe, you may find yourself unable to perform these necessary tasks. This can lead to consequences up to and including losing your job.

People who have social phobias also have a higher than normal risk of developing conditions such as depression or other anxiety disorders. This is likely due to the feelings of isolation that can progressively develop at a specific time. Another possible reason is that some people seem to be hardwired for anxiety, which can manifest in a wide range of ways.

Physical symptoms of Glossophobia

- Sweating
- Increased heart rate
- Dry mouth
- Difficulty breathing
- Nausea
- Headache
- Muscle tension
- Need to take a bio break (Toilets)

Successful Treatment Options

Glossophobia can be successfully treated in a variety of possible ways. One of the most common is cognitive-behavioral therapy (CBT). You will learn to replace your messages of fear with more positive self-talk. You will also learn relaxation techniques and what to do when you experience a panic attack. You will gradually confront your fear in a safe and controlled environment.

Medications may also be prescribed to gently help you get control of your generous fear. Medication is generally used in conjunction with therapy rather than on its own.

Once you have successfully worked through the worst of your fear, you might want to consider joining speaking groups that can help you polish your public speaking skills through repetition and constructive criticism from fellow members. Building confidence in your ability to speak in public can further reduce your anxiety.

Social Anxiety Disorder SAD

The reasons for Glossophobia range from apprehension delivered by an absence of planning to, perhaps the most well known mental disorder, Social Anxiety Disorder SAD.

Its side effects shift from physiological changes, mental disruptions, and adverse speech performance. There are a few different ways to conquer Glossophobia, which incorporate arrangement and practising, deconstructing your convictions, taking part in positive self-talk, visualizing your ideal performance, rehearsing care, breathing exercises, making an anxiety pecking order, utilizing augmented reality, automated mentors and drugs, for example, beta-blockers

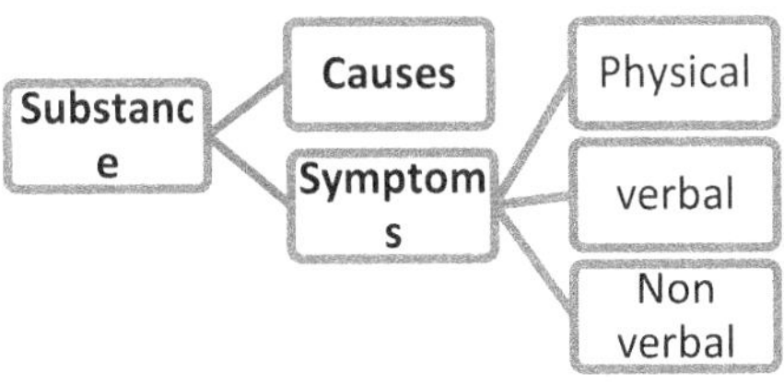

Substance

1   Causes
2   Symptoms

Causes

This part needs extra references for the check. Kindly assistance improves this article by adding references to dependable sources. Un-sourced material might be tested and eliminated.

Glossophobia, otherwise called public speaking anxiety and speech anxiety, is a fear of speaking in public. These tensions are a particular indication of social anxiety delivered by fearfulness identified with the Fight-or-flight reaction, which is created by an apparent threat; this triggers a raised safeguard response in the Sympathetic sensory system to be ready, to run, stow away or freeze. It is connected to the mental condition known as Social anxiety Disorder SAD a psychological predisposition to accept that social collaborations will bring about brutal negative judgment from others and poor results on account of such judgement; hence, before the social cooperation happens, for example, a public speech, the individual makes negative considerations of disappointment, dread and being unable, creating negative sentiments and physiological responses.

People who experience the ill effects of SAD participate in pessimistic visualization and self-talk which ends their consideration and capacity to remain centred and channel their intellectual force and actual energy.

Individuals experiencing SAD accept they are simply bad at public speaking, setting a conviction as a reality and succumbing to a mainstream mental marvel known as Self-satisfying prediction Moreover, people with SAD add more mental pressing factor because of the way that they normally anticipate that others should like them or acknowledge them, measure their self-esteem by their social cooperation performance, and accept that indicating feelings is equivalent to demonstrating weakness.

Moreover, other key reasons for this anxiety have been recognized as the oddity of the experience, the characteristics of the audience, the figment of straightforwardness and how much the speaker distinguishes public speaking as a performance rather than a demonstration of communication.

Symptoms

The more explicit manifestations of speech anxiety can be gathered into three categories:

1. Physical
2. Verbal
3. Non-verbal

Physical Symptoms: Actual side effects include shaking, perspiring, butterflies in the stomach, dry mouth, and quick heartbeats expanded sweat and oxygen consumption, solidifying of neck/upper back muscles, and dry mouth. The wild shaking is additionally normal and often happens prior to the fear-inspiring upgrade.

Verbal manifestations: It incorporates (however, are not restricted to) a strained or shuddering voice, and expressed stops known as vocal fillers.

Nonverbal: These indications could incorporate going clear during the speech and staying reliant on note cards.

Chapter-2

Celebrities those having Stage Fear

Confidence does not come when you have all the answers, but it comes when you are ready to face all the Questions

One of the significant worries of us is stage fear or fright. We should confront the issue solidly. In the event that you feel  anxious or nervous about giving a speech, you are in generally excellent company of people. Most prominent public speakers in history have experienced stage fear or shyness that includes Rowan Sebastian Atkinson (Mr. Bean), Abraham Lincoln, Indian Bollywood star Amitabh Bachhan, Winston Churchill and many.

Most of the people who deal and conserves effectively in all sorts of regular circumstances become frightened / scared to face the audience to make a speech. In the event that you are stressed over stage fright, you may feel better realizing that you are not alone.

Inspiration case study -Abraham Lincoln

"Unpublished 1860 letter by Abraham Lincoln Shows 'Nervous' Side"

The latest headline is frightening or startling: **"Unpublished 1860 letter by Abraham Lincoln Shows 'Nervous' Side."** In addition, if that does not astound you, this may: Lincoln uncovers in the letter that public speaking is the reason for his nervousness.

Do the most prominent speakers truly experience the ill effects of stage fright, very much like so many of us do today? The appropriate answer seems, by all accounts, to be yes . . . furthermore, the news contains significant exercise for us all who speak in public. You must be dynamic instead of a nervous speaker.

Speech Anxiety: A Mix of Visibility and Vulnerability

Lincoln composed the letter on March 6, 1860, after he had conveyed a high-profile speech at Cooper

Union, the science and Arts College in New York City. His speech, on the need to control the spread of slavery to the territories, an "electrifying" effect on his audience. Indeed, the speech Lincoln onto the public stage—much more so than the popular Lincoln-Douglas discusses-was given two years earlier. Furthermore, that, it appears, is the means by which stage fright entered the image. Following the Cooper Union talk, a Republican political panel to speak in New Jersey welcomed Lincoln. In the letter, Lincoln rejected that invitation, calling himself "nervous and unfit" to fill a speaking commitment previously made in Connecticut. Lincoln, at the end of the day, is encountering an exemplary manifestation of "class symptoms of speech anxiety: the blend of permeability and weakness.

Here is the full Note from Lincoln

Yours of the second was received late last evening. I cannot speak in New Jersey this time. I have over staid my time—have heard something about sickness in my family—and really am nervous and unfit to fill my engagement already made here in Connecticut. Will you please excuse me?

Yours Respectfully,A. Lincoln

(Source: Mailonline /dailymail.co.uk)

Lincoln's Example of How to Deal with Stage Fright

You or I presumably will not be speaking about America's personality to a public audience. However, we can take in learning notes something significant from our most prominent speaker concerning how to manage stage fright. Lincoln was a Lawyer, overall. However, Lincoln gives us a strong message how to manage and overcome speech anxiety.

To Overcome Fear of Public Speaking that Lincoln was an extraordinary speechwriter; yet in this speech, he plays it plain and straight. There are no expository twists

Lincoln is just attempting to make himself clear, address the clear message across, using simple language, language that is straightforward and difficult to deny. As such, he has not tried to deliver a great presentation or give a speech. As such, he is making an effort not to convey an awakening speech or an incredible presentation. His audience and the focuses he is making is the entirety of his core interest. There's no room left for buying into all that "visibility and vulnerability."

Furnished with the right focus on his audience and message, Abraham Lincoln need not have stressed that he was ill suited / unfit as a speaker. A similar immovable focus will work well for you in the event that you have stage fear (fright), anyway humble or groundbreaking your own message.

The source of inspiration for the story of Abraham Lincoln is from abrahamlincolnonline.org, Fox news. And the genard method websites

Inspiration case study: two
Rowan Sebastian Atkinson

"But unfortunately, speaking disorder stopped him, but he created a history in the Television & Film Industry, has a total asset assessed to be $130 million "

He is an actor, writer and comedian. He is famous for acting characters well known as **Mr. Bean & Blackadder**. He is also part of the world-renowned movie **"The lion king, Johnny English** and he is listed as one of the 50 funniest actors in British comedy.

Mr. Bean (Rowan Atkinson) was born in a middle-class family whose father was a farmer. He was a hard worker, so got admission to Oxford University. One of his teachers said, "Nothing was outstanding about him. I didn't expect him to become a fantastic scientist." He proved everybody wrong by being admitted at Oxford University. During his days in Oxford, he was falling in love with acting. In the acting filed, everyone required speaking abilities. However, unfortunately, speaking disorder stopped him. He continues his master's degree in Electrical Engineering.

After graduating with a Master's degree, he decided to complete his dream by becoming an actor. Therefore, he enrols in a comedy group, but again his stammering got in the way.

He got rejections from various TV shows. Still, he never stopped believing in himself. He had a great passion for making people laugh, and he knew it. Therefore, he starts creating original comedy sketches. Rowan Atkinson realizes that whenever he plays some character, he can speak fluently. He used it as an inspiration for his acting.

He started taking interest in acting and were enrolled in a comedy group, but he could not perform well due to his speaking disorder. Despite all the hardships, he still believed in himself. Still, he kept being rejected because he did not have a good face and a grand body. Then, he proved everyone wrong!

Mr. Rowan Atkinson began his own show "Mr. Bean", which turned into a worldwide SUCCESS. Today, Rowan Atkinson is one of the most well known famous people ever and has a total assets is assessed to be $130 million. Rowan Atkinson Success Story instructs us that: For progress, you needn't bother with a lovely face and courageous body all you need is Passion to overcome the limitations and Hard Work with these two Secret of Success you can accomplish anything you desire.

Inspiration case study: three
Amitabh Bachhan

Star of the Millennium – acted in more than 200 Indian films, National & International Awards winner.

Amitabh Bachhan an Indian film famous actor, filmmaker, TV host, occasional playback artist, singer and former politician. He is viewed as one of the best and most powerful actor throughout the entire history of Indian cinema. The French director François Truffaut considered him a "one-man industry"

"Most prominent entertainer of the century", Star of the Millennium, or Big B, he has since shown up in more than 200 Indian films in a vocation spreading over more than five decades and has won various honours in his profession, including four National Film Awards as Best Actor, Dadasaheb Phalke Award as lifetime accomplishment grant and numerous honors at global film celebrations and grant services.

He has won sixteen Filmfare Awards and is the most named entertainer in any significant acting class at Filmfare, with 42 selections in general. He has hosted as an anchor for the game show Kaun Banega Crorepati, India's adaptation of the game show establishment, Who Wants to Be a Millionaire. He additionally entered governmental issues for a period during the 1980s.

The Government of India honoured Mr. Bachhan with the Padma Shri in 1984, the Padma Bhushan in 2001 and the Padma Vibhushan in 2015 for his commitments to human expressions. The Government of France regarded him with its most elevated non-military personnel honour, Knight of the Legion of honour, in 2007 for his outstanding vocation in the realm of film and past. Bachhan additionally showed up in a Hollywood film.

Role model enlighten us to overcome from Stage fear

As per the source from **ZEE news** uploaded on 1ˢᵗ June 2015 at 13:58 hours

Appearances before public are frightening

https://moola66652.zeenews.india.com/entertainment/celebrity/appearances-before-public-are-frightening-amitabh-bachchan_1602425.html

Dear readers, Mr.Amithab Bachhan is the most respectful Indian icon. **He is enriching us to overcome the stage fear**. He is one of role models, his achievements, awards, personal ethics, values, philosophy, helping nature and very humble Indian is motivating that stage fear cannot stop your success.

The author of this book is having very high regard, respect and honour towards him. Taking his inspiration, we can overcome the stage fear. In these case studies, we should take a positive note and develop our positive thoughts to improve our public speaking skills and avoid the "Stage Fear".

Chapter-3

Mind-set & Approaches

"Do not fear failure but rather fear not trying."
— *Roy T. Bennett,*

A student and his coach were walking in the mountains. Suddenly, his student was scared to see the deep forest, tall mountains, while climbing the mountain student falls, injures himself and screams: "ooohhh! "To his surprise, he overhears the echoing voice repeating, somewhere in the mountain: "ooohhh!"

To test this, the student shouts at first time: "Who are you?"
He receives the answer: "Who are you?"
A student shouts a second time: I am scared
He receives the echoing answer: I am scared
Third-time student screams to the mountain:
"I admire you!"
The voice answers: "I admire you!

He considers his coach and asks: "What's going on?" The coach smiles and says: "My student, pay attention."

This time Coach shouts:" You are a champion!" The voice answers: "You are a champion!"

"People call this ECHO, but really this is LIFE. It gives you back everything you give, take, or do. Our life is simply a reflection of our actions. If you says you are having stage fear, you will face stage fear, if you say that you are great public speaker, you will become a public speaker, if you want more love in the world; create more love in your heart. This relationship applies to everything, in all aspects of life.

Dear readers trust the author, after reading & practising the techniques mentioned in this book will help you to overcome the stage fear and become an effective public speaker.

Life will give you back everything you have given to it. Overcoming from stage fear and offers, the opportunity to change lives all time to improve things.

The accomplishment of success in any movement will be a result of the psychological edge with which you approach it. A Forbes article composed by a psychotherapist and mental strength writer expresses that "thoughts are a catalyst for self-perpetuating cycles" This holds particularly valid for public speaking.

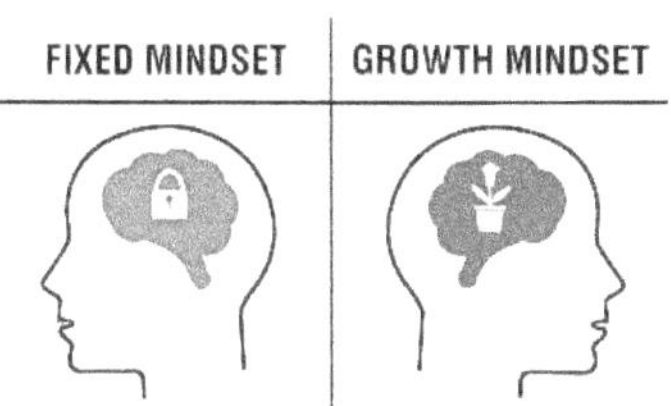

The approaches of public speaking on the stage will be two types of approaches.

1. Positive mind-set on stage
2. Negative mind-set on stage

1. Positive mind-set on stage:-

Having optimistic thoughts to overcome stage fear and public speaking methods. An example of this mind-set is *"I can do this. There is no speech, which I cannot deal with. I am confident that I have prepared the speech well and delivered the same on the stage.*

On this regard, during this event if any unintentional error or made a mistake. What will be a Positive person immediate reaction?

-   Its okay, it is not going to end the universe.

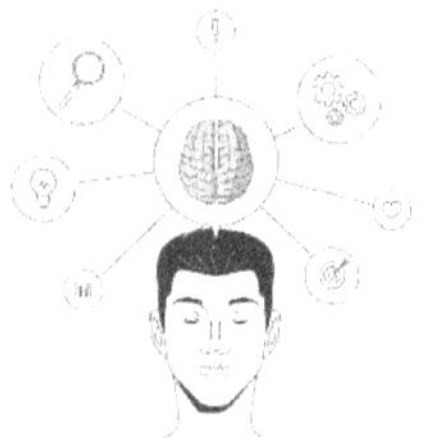

I will correct and continue to improve.

- This improvement cannot come overnight; it will come through continuous practice. Even if there will be errors during the practice on stage, its okay, errors will be corrected.
- Self will realize the mistakes on stage and take a learning note from them in a sportive manner that self will not repe at the same next time.
- Next time, it is optimistic there will be a chance for the next time.
- I am not apprehensive or nervous because in light of the fact that I dread disappointment, however energized for the chance of opportunity to encounter achievement.
- I do not fear disappointment / failure. I realize that disappointment does not actually exist. Disappointment is just last, in the event that I acknowledge it all things considered.
- I never carry past mistakes, criticism for my stage performance.
- I have the skills to do this. This is another progression on the excursion of dominating public speaking and I will succeed and push ahead.

Negative mind-set on stage

Then again, shortage-based thoughts are

- Can i do this?
- I am not confident to this speech on stage can deal with this speech anymore.
- Did I prepare and plan well enough?
- I do not know whether I have confidence in my preparation and myself.
- What in the event that I commit an error or mistake on stage?
- What in the event that I commit two errors? What in the event that I fail on stage in front of the public?
- Self will have his own talents and start underestimating his own public speaking skills.

Thoughts resemble fights, and attitudes of mind-set are war. The fights between the two kinds of thoughts will decide the result of this battle.

Practice Winston Churchill Quotes

"Success is not final, failure is not fatal: it is the courage to continue that counts"

Chapter-4

Psychometric Test

"Raise your actions, not voice. It is a rain that grows flowers, not thunder"

Psychometric tests are a norm and logical technique, a scientific and systematic method used to assess people's psychological capacities and social-behavioural style. Psychometric tests are intended to design the necessary character attributes and inclination (or intellectual capacities).

> - If you would like to know the height of yourself and then the observer will tell weight and not disclose height, will that, be acceptable to you?
> - If do you have an examination of mathematics and even though if you mentioned correct chemistry formulas & concepts of chemistry, do you succeed to clear the mathematics examination?
> - If you are suffering from hair fall and if you will take medication for diarrhoea, do you cure the disease?

The results are not positive. It indicates **diagnosing is very important** before further proceedings. It will be applicable to overcome stage fear also.

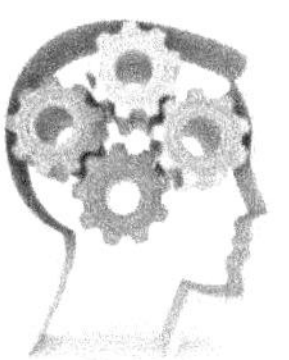

It is important to know our strengths, weakness, opportunities and threats as a public speaker. TMAS will help to rate our anxiety, for this subject we can considered in terms of stage fear. It recognizes the degree to which you are having stage fear intellectual capacities match those needed to play out.

The Taylor Manifest Anxiety Scale (TMAS) is a test of anxiety will that will help to measure the public speaker personality trait on stage or any other platform. It is an anxiety psychometric test as a personality trait and was made by Ms. Janet Taylor in 1953 to identify the subjects who might be valuable in the investigation of anxiety disorders. The Taylor Manifest Anxiety Scale, often abbreviated to TMAS, is an anxiety psychometric test as a personality trait and was made by Ms. Janet Taylor in 1953 to identify the subjects who might be valuable in the investigation of anxiety disorders.

The IMAS initially comprised 50 True or False questions, which individuals answer by thinking about themselves, to decide their anxiety level. The statements below inquiring about your behaviour and emotions will imply to the public speaker also. Consider each statement carefully.

Then indicate whether the statements are generally true or false for you.

Particulars

1. I do not tire quickly   [   ]
2. I believe I am no more nervous than others   [   ]
3. I have very few headaches   [   ]
4. I work under a great deal of tension   [   ]
5. I frequently notice my hand shakes
    when I try do something   [   ]
6. I blush no more often than others   [   ]
7. I have diarrhea one a month or more   [   ]
8. I worry quite a bit over possible misfortunes [   ]
9. I practically never blush   [   ]
10. I am often afraid that I am going to blush   [   ]
11. My hands and feet are usually warm enough [   ]
12. I sweat very easily even on cool days   [   ]
13. Sometimes when embarrassed,
    I break out in a sweat   [   ]
14. I hardly ever notice my heart pounding,
        and I am seldom short of breath   [   ]
15. I feel hungry almost all of the time   [   ]
16. I am very seldom troubled by constipation   [   ]
17. I have a great deal of stomach trouble   [   ]
18. I have had minor health issues,
    in which I lost sleep over worry   [   ]
19. I am easily embarrassed   [   ]
20. I am more sensitive than most other people [   ]
21. I frequently find myself worrying
    about something   [   ]

22. I wish I be as happy as others seem to be   [   ]
23. I am usually calm and not easily upset   [   ]

24. I feel anxiety about something
    or someone almost all of the time   [   ]
25. I am happy most of the time   [   ]
26. It makes me nervous to have to wait   [   ]
27. Sometimes I become so excited
    I find it hard to get to sleep   [   ]
28. I have sometimes felt that difficulties piling
    up so high I couldn't get over them   [   ]
29. I admit I have felt worried beyond reason
    over small things   [   ]
30. I have very few fears compared to my friends[   ]
31. I certainly feel useless at times   [   ]
32. I find it hard to keep my mind on a task or job [   ]
33. I am usually self-conscious   [   ]
34. I am inclined to take things hard   [   ]
35. At times I think I am no good at all   [   ]
36. I am certainly lacking in self-confidence   [   ]
37. I sometimes feel that-
    I am about to go to pieces   [   ]
38. I am entirely self-confident   [   ]

Scoring procedure:

1. If the overall score lie between 0 and 25, then the individual is having low anxiety

2. If the overall score lies between 26 and 50, then the individual having high anxiety.

Chapter-5

Biggest Fear in the Life

"Don't give up – The hardest battles are given to the strongest solders"

Actually, most people tend to be anxious before doing something important in public. Actors are nervous before a play, politicians are nervous before a campaign speech, athletes are nervous before a big game. The ones who succeed have learned to use their nervousness to their advantage. Listen to the stage fright

> A 2001 Gallup Poll asked that Americans list their greatest fears. 40% Identified speaking before the audience, a gathering as their top fear, surpassed simply by the 51% who said they feared snakes.

> A 2005 survey reviews almost similar outcomes, with 42% of respondents being responded by the possibility of speaking in public. In

correlation, just 28% said they feared passing on. In an alternate report, researchers focused on social situations and once more, conducting questions on their subjects list their biggest fears.

In excess of 9,000 people were interviewed. Here is the positioning of their answers: seven Biggest Fears. Once more, speech making is at the top in inciting anxiety.

1. Public speaking
2. Speaking up in a meeting or class
3. Meeting new people
4. Talking to people in authority
5. Important examination or interview
6. Going to parties
7. Talking with strangers

Chapter -6

Techniques to Overcome Stage Fear

No poison can kill a Positive thinker and No medicine can cure a Negative Thinker

Execution uneasiness and stage fear remain very standard wonders that happen to numerous people. Stage fright or performance anxiety in common is a persistent phobia that is naturally roused in a unique individual when required to carefully perform in front of an audience.

There is a peculiar sensation frequently experienced in the presence of an audience. It might continue from the look of the numerous eyes that turn upon the speaker, particularly on the off chance that he allows himself to consistently return that look. Most speakers have been aware of this adventure, a genuine something, infesting the environment, substantial, transitory, incredible.

Practice, practice, Practice in speaking before an audience will in general eliminate all fears of audiences, Stage fright or performance anxiety represent the fear a person feels when he or she is required to perform in some way.

Overcoming from Stage fear

Instead of trying to eliminate each mark of stage fear, you should transform in to positive thoughts changing it from negative power into positive thoughts "an enthusiastic, energetic, lively feeling etc. It's still nervousness, yet it feels like an extraordinary difference.

Avoid thinking that you are having stage fear. Try not to consider yourself having anxiety in front of large audiences. Instead of this consider yourself as "Stage excitement" or "Stage Enthusiasm".

Reading & practising the following techniques or formulas will help you to overcome from "Stage Fear" .

Technique. No. 1

Positive Thinking

Things won't better unless you think better

Self-confidence is a notable force of positive thinking. In the event that you think you can do it, you can. Then again, in the event that you predict the worst situation of destruction that is quite often what you will get. This is especially true when it comes to public speaking. Speakers who contemplate themselves with negative thoughts may not overcome stage fear than speakers who think positively. Here are a few different ways you can change negative thoughts into positive ones as you work on your speeches:

Negative Thoughts	Positive thoughts
I don't want to give this speech	Giving speech is chance for self to transform ideas, knowledge and get into experience as best public speaker.
I am not effective public speaker	None of us perfect, but getting betterment for each speech.
I am always stressed and nervous, when i would like impart the speech	If other people can overcome the nervousness and do it, i can also do it with my speech
None of the audience will be interested in my speech, what i want to explain	I am having best topic and completely prepared, surely audience will be interested.

Technique. No. 2

Power of Visualization

Imaination is more important than knowledge - Albert Einstein

Visualization is a firmly identified with positive reasoning. Artists, entertainers, speakers, sports persons and others to improve their performance in stressful situations utilize it.

The way to visualization is making a clear psychological blueprint in which you see yourself succeeding prevailing in your speech. Visualize yourself in your bit auditorium and addressing a huge crowd ascending to deliver a speech. See yourself at the podium, ready and confident, making eye contact with your audience and conveying your presentation in a firm, clear, vibrant voice.

Feel your confidence developing as your audience members get their attention & participate what you are saying. Envision your pride as you close the speech realizing you have done your absolute best. As you make these pictures to your thought process, be practical; yet keep on track with the positive parts of your speech. Try not to permit negative pictures to dominate the positive ones.

Recognize your nervousness; however, visualize yourself overcoming it to give a dynamic presentation. In the speech event that one part of the speech give you inconvenience, visualize yourself overcoming that without any controversies.

Also, be explicit and focus on specific objectives. The more clear your psychological pictures are, the more effective you are probably going to be. Similarly as with your physical practice of speech, this sort of psychological practice ought to be rehashed a few times a long time before you speak. It does not guarantee that each speech will turn as you imagine. However, utilized related with different strategies for fighting anxiety in front of large audiences, it is a demonstrated method to help control your nerves and create an effective presentation.

Technique. No.3

Gentle gestures of Hands

The people who succeed are not the ones who avoid failure; they are the ones who learn how to respond to failure with optimism.

Gestures are very important. The motion will give a replica to the audience that you do not have any stage fear and you are addressing them in a professional and friendly manner. If you tie your hands on  stage, it gives a message you are having stage fear.

On top of your voice projection, the certainty of self-confidence level and capacity to empower the audience, hand gestures can help your speech and makes the audience more interested in the thing you are saying. Hand gestures, can assist to make the talking environment dynamic. With these gestures, different talkers can know your feelings. This can make the discussion easily. Hand gestures can assist to others with understanding speaker core points rapidly. A great talk utilizes their gestures to tell the audience 'this is the main thing I need to say '. Hand gestures or body gestures can help you talk smoothly with the audience who communicate in different dialects.

Technique. No. 4

Incorporate humour

A day without laughter is a day wasted
- Charlie Chaplin

In the course of history, three main humour theories emerged,
We laugh when we feel superior

- We laugh when something surprisingly causes us to change our perspective.
- Humour serves to dissolve psychological tensions and to reveal suppressed desires.

Knowing when to utilize humour is fundamental. So is building up the comedic timing to convey it with the most prominent impact.

- Humour makes a connection between the speaker and the audience.
- It empowers individuals and keeps them attentive
- Humour can give emotional, passionate relief.
- It assists the audience with recollecting your focuses.
- Humour frequently makes the speaker more receptive, approachable, and agreeable.
- Humour assists individuals with recollecting things better.

Technique. No. 5

Make maximum moments on Stage

"Success is our own shadow. Don't try to catch it walk your own way, it will automatically follow you. Remind shadow follows you only when you walk towards brightness"

In theatre and performing shows, expressions, the stage will be called a deck alluded stagecraft is an assigned, designed space for the performance of creations. The stage fills in as space for actors or entertainers and a point of convergence (the screen in film theatres) for the crowd.

To avoid stage fear, utilize maximum moments on the stage. Both the corners and middle space of the Stage are frequently touched.

Technique. No.6

Don't blink your eyes on Stage

Eye contact can reveal if a person is, shy or gregarious. Honest or deceitful, confident or terrified. Interested or bored. Patient or irritated. Sincere or inauthentic, organized or unprepared. Attentive of distracted. - Susan C Young

Being a speaker, you are addressing the audience. Due to stage fear, if you keep on blinking your eyes and not concentrating the audience, this is not a good symptom.

"Great speakers find a way of making an early connection with their audience. It can be as simple as walking confidently on stage, looking around, making eye contact with two or three people and smiling" - Chris Anderson

"Not every President is a great speaker. Not every President is a great thinker. But in the modern era, every single President is a master of one thing: eye contact."
— Brad Meltzer

Technique. No. 7

Try not to fight your Stage fight…work with it

Everyone gets stage fright. Embrace it and make it work for you or it will work against you - Ruth Sherman

You need to expect and acknowledge the way that you will feel on edge, particularly the initial couple of moments of your introduction.

The more you oppose your nervousness, the more it will neutralize you. Once more, centre on the introduction when speaking in public, the tension will gradually dial down.

Tips to work with it

- ✓ Relax before you talk.
- ✓ Practise your talk until you are familiar.
- ✓ Write down your worries and action plans to overcome them.
- ✓ Keep your top three fears.
- ✓ Watch something funny to make you laugh.
- ✓ Visualize your ideal performance.

Technique. No. 8

Research your Topic

Genius is one percent inspiration and ninety-nine percent perspiration. I have not failed. I have just found 10,000 ways that will not work. – Thomas A Edison

Good speakers stick to what they know. Incredible speakers research what they need to pass on their message. The prime step of any speaker to avoid the stage fear is the right selection of topic. If the research topic has not been done appropriately, the speaker will often having a fear what to speak on the stage.

- ✓ Research is an apparatus for building information and working with learning. It is a way to get issues and increment public mindfulness.
- ✓ It deals with facts and figures
- ✓ Encouraging basic reasoning, critical thinking and logical abilities hands on learning.
- ✓ Characterizing scholastic, profession and individual interests
- ✓ Growing information and comprehension of a picked field outside of the homeroom
- ✓ Creating one-on-one associations with recognized personnel in their field
- ✓ Building people group with companions, personnel and associations on-and off-grounds

Technique. No.9

Avoid visual interruptions

You can only win when your mind is stronger than your emotions.

One of the most effective tools for the speech to overcome stage fear is the visual presentation. If any interruptions during your presentation are, made speaker may might be nervous. However, please be cool.....If the interruption is a visual one, I suggest acknowledging it only if other people have also seen it. If it is something you alone have spotted, you can choose to ignore it.

- The human eye naturally seeks simplicity and clarity. If you clutter your PowerPoint slides with an abundance of text and graphics, you will confuse viewers and lose their attention.

- When you read a book, magazine or newspaper, you usually see black text on a white background. This formula is pleasing to the eye and increases readability.

- While adding some transitions is fine, be sure that they serve a purpose such as directing viewer attention to a certain portion of the slide. Do not use transitions or animations just because you can. Overuse of these catchy features makes for a presentation that seems all too cliché.

Technique. No.10

Proper Hands moments

"Let your handshake be a greater bond than any written contract."— *Steve Maraboli,*

One of the stage fear symptom is hiding hands and covering body behind the podium. Hence, "Ensure to exhibit your palms of your hands facing the audience" .How much you use open hands, that much you're so confident and you will impart the speech above your expectation. Have hands moments, do not tie or hide your hands during your presentation.

- Have you ever thought about how your hands — and what you do with them when you speak in front of an audience
- DO pay attention to where your hands are and what you are doing with them.
- DO use your hands in a manner that conveys confidence.
- DO NOT wring your hands because that tells the audience (rightly or wrongly) that you are nervous or worried and possibly unsure about what you are saying.
- DO use your hands to convey emotion.

Technique. No.11

Never Under estimate

"Remember no one can make you feel inferior without your consent." - Eleanor Roosevelt

Don't underestimate yourself and audience Regardless of whether you are a world-known master in your specialized topic, it is as yet not a smart thought to utilize phrases like "this is presumably new to you" or "you most likely don't have the foggiest idea what this implies", except if you are sharing historic news that no one has known about.

Effective tips to overcome from the inferiority feeling

- Challenge your negative thoughts
- Note your positive traits
- Stop unhelpful insults or criticism
- Increase your self-esteem
- Practice regular heath routines
- Focus on your goal
- periodical reassessing underestimation

Technique. No.12

Don't rush it for the Self introduction & speech

Many problems in the world would disappear if we talked to each other instead of about each other.

Try not to rush your introduction. Start moderate and permit yourself an opportunity to get into an agreeable speed. You need time to become accustomed to the audience and the audience additionally needs an ideal opportunity to become accustomed to you. A self-introduction and topic clarify what your identity is, your main event and what others need to think about you. Because of stage tension, if the speaker scrambles for his or her self-presentation and different points in the show, they miss the expert methodology. The advantages of effective self-introduction are as follows

- ✓ Builds a favourable impression.
- ✓ Positive thinking.
- ✓ Sharpens presentation skills.
- ✓ Enhances the ability to meet people.
- ✓ It helps build connections.
- ✓ Enhances self-confidence.
- ✓ Deep understanding.
- ✓ Generated motivation.

Technique. No. 13

Never be Shy

Train your mind to see the good in everything. Positively is a choice. The happiness of your life depends on the quality of your thoughts.

A quarter of the time, nobody will see you are anxious. Why should you should advise your shyness to them? You may feel yourself shaking and shuddering. However, your audience probably will not know about it.

Try it also . It will make your audience apprehensive as well and they will be too stressed over your exhibition to get much out of your introduction.

Techniques to overcome from shyness

- ✓ There's no need to advertise your shyness
- ✓ Change your tone
- ✓ Avoid bullies and teases
- ✓ Practice placing yourself in not-so-comfortable situations
- ✓ Remember that one bad moment doesn't mean a bad day
- ✓ Record your progress and proceed further

Technique. No.14

Stand straight & don't bend your shoulders

Effective communication is 20% what you know and 80% how you feel about what you know. ~ Jim

Body language will explain so many things to others. If the speaker is under stress on stage, he might tilt his body to one side or bend the shoulders. To avoid this nervousness, please stand straight and do not bend your shoulders in front of the audience.

Technique. No.15

Act & Talk morally

Without a moral compass, the human mind will justify anything. Mehrnaz Bassiri

Since public speaking apprehensions are so normal, understand the colossal force of impact that you hold.

Ethical public speaking is no a single occasion. Ethical public speaking is a systematic process. This cycle starts when you start conceptualizing the subject of your discourse.

Technique. No.16

Eliminate fear of rejection

The fear of rejection is worse than rejection itself. Truth is like a surgery, it hurts, but it heals. A lie is like a painkiller; it gives instant relief, but has side effects forever.

To become a fearless speaker, it is significant that you should remove the myth "Fear of Rejection" from your brain. The fear of rejection is an unreasonable fear that has you persuaded that people will not acknowledge or endorse you because of your sentiments, looks, character, values, qualities, personality, beliefs or conduct.

The vast majority experience a few nerves while putting themselves in circumstances that could prompt rejection, however people, the fear gets devastating. This fear can have numerous basic causes.

- False representation
- People-Pleasing
- Passivity
- Disappointment etc.

Technique. No.17

Relaxation on Intervals.

Learn to relax. Your body is precious, as it houses your mind and spirit. -Norman Vincent Peale

To overcome stage fear, one of the best techniques that Public speakers practice on & off the stage is practicing 'relaxation' during intervals. Relaxation is fundamental to overcome stress. At the point when we relax, the progression of blood increments around our body, giving us more energy.

It assists us with having a more settled and clearer brain, which helps with positive reasoning, fixation, memory and dynamic. Minutes before you go in front of an audience, take some slow & full breaths, so that when you get to the stage your breathing will be all right. Rehearsing relaxation procedures can have numerous advantages, including:

- Slowing heart rate
- Reduce the stage fear, anger & frustration.
- Bringing down the blood pressure
- slowly controlling breathing rate
- Keeping up normal sugar level
- blood flow to significant muscles
- Improving concentration and mood
- Improving rest quality
- Bringing down weakness

Technique. No.18

Exhibit confidence & steadiness

If you want to find the truth, do not listen to the words coming to you. Rather see the body language of the speaker. It speaks the facts not audible. - Bhavas Chhatbar

Self-confidence and fearless is a mind-set which comes from within, and it is achievable for all of us. At the point when you talk, you do not simply talk what you really say. The speaker must speak a firm body language. From your looks, to your stance, expression, posture, eye contact they  all will get consider the 'truth' behind the thing you are saying. In case you are feeling nervous, your body could be giving an alternate message to your audience than the one you are saying.

Employees, investors, and partners do not simply follow anyone — they follow leaders who have command of the business and command of the stage. Speaker being judged on his confidence and competence, not just your content, and the way you appear and how you sound matters.

Technique. No.19

Know that most nervousness will not visible

Nervous & excited are the same sensation. Negative Vs Positive. Stop saying you are nervous and start saying you are excited. -Deb Bixler

I realize that most nervousness is not visible.Numerous beginner speakers are stressed  over seeming apprehensive to the audience. It is difficult to speak with balance and ensure confirmation in the event that you think you look tense and not secure. Quite possibly the most significant exercises you will learn as your speech class continues "Your sensory system might be giving you 1,000 shocks," says one of the great speakers, "but the viewer can see only a few of them.

Despite the fact that your palms are sweating and your heart is high beating, your audience members likely will not understand how tense you are—particularly on the off chance that you do your best to act cool and certain outwardly.

Technique. No.20

Chin-up while giving speech

Chin-up, keep moving at your own pace. For, life is a marathon, Not race – Subiya

Keep your chin &head held high. Keeping your head high symbolizes that you are confident on stage. Here keeping head high means not looking sealing.

Understand what your standard face resembles. This is the face that the audience see when you are see them, tuning in to them or simply not talking when all is said and done.

Technique. No.21

Use Complement words with visual guides

I take compliments and I take constructive criticism. Not everyone loves you. You react the way as a footballer. I use it all to make me play better. -Timothy

Exchanging of complimentary words will make the speaker more comfortable and avoids stage fear. Complimentary words are those that we use in communication because the individual we are conversing with to has a positive and good outlook on himself or herself.

They are for the most part words to depict a part of someone's character/life or to portray something that has a place with the individual getting the commendation. It goes far in building rapport, compatibility with the individual you are conversing with. Your capacity to quickly and timely complement during your communications. Getting praises is the other portion of the social show that you need to continue to keep up correspondence in the interchanges.

Technique. No.22

Use your voice successfully

Do not let the noise of others opinions drown out your own inner voice - Steve Jobs

Probably the greatest stage fear the vast majority have when they are approached to talk publicly includes their voices. The concern often includes how our voices sound.

There is a simple path not to stress over that issue. Practically nobody prefers his or her own voice when he or she hears it played back.

It sounds not the same as the manner in which we hear it when we are speaking, and that will in general trouble individuals. Hence, practice voice bases accordingly. You might be having stage fear, but manage with your voice modulation. Tone using breaking rapport will boost your confidence & attraction in the public. Remember to modulate your voice according to your message.

Technique. No.23

Exhibit confidence, no matter what?

With confidence, you have won before you have started.
~ Marcus Garvey

Kindly remember, stage fear is a faction of minutes or a couple of speeches. Once you are overcome, there are no boundaries for you. Even during your speech if you were struck, do not stop your speech and exhibit self-confidence.

Speaker confidence levels will grow as you go from speaking to small groups of people up to large audiences. This will benefit you not just on stage, but also in everyday personal and professional life.

Few tips to boost your confidence

- Talk positively to your self
- Stake a power pose
- Reframe your nervousness as excitement'
- Meet and greet the audience before your presentation
- Smile

Technique. No.24

Use Pictures

Photography is an art of observation. It has little to do with the things you see and everything to do with the way you see them. Elliott Erwitt

Utilization of graphic or pictorial representation that might include a photograph of you on the first slide to personalise your presentation.

- Use visuals or images that first support your content, and then add to the aesthetic value of the slide.
- Images are used to tell the story of your slide, Saves you time when creating your presentation
- Makes your presentation more effective and engaging
- Helps your career (by gaining a reputation as an effective communicator)
- Pictures increases the likelihood of audience
- Visuals help audiences remember the material
- Helps your audience understand the presentation material
- Pay attention to you
- Visuals resonate with audiences and inspire people to act

Technique. No.25

Know yourself, content & Audience

*Knowing yourself is the beginning of all wisdom -
Aristotle*

As a speaker, you must know about your talents, specialities of the content and your audience demands. These principles will help you to overcome the stage fear.

Nothing will stop in its tracks like being ready. Know your substance, your discourse and all the more critically your audience. In the event that you understand what you are discussing, at that point you are motivated to be apprehensive. Understanding your topic subject will empower you to talk more normally and consequently, more unhesitatingly. Likewise, should a specialized hitch happen, this will not upset you, as you are now sure regarding the matter.

Technique. No.26

Utilize nonverbal communication

Nonverbal communication is an elaborate secret code that is written nowhere, known by none, and understood by all. Edward Sapir

Non-verbal communication is the systematic cycle of communication through sending and getting (for the most part apparent) signals between individuals. Nonverbal  communications is available in the vast majority of relational discussions, incorporating communication with the utilization of emoji's. Nonverbal communications pass on more information than verbal communication.

- ✓ It saves time in communication.
- ✓ It is fast in getting feedback once conveyed.
- ✓ It gives total comprehension of communication conveyed, and there is an opportunity to make it even more clearly in the event of questions in understanding of words or thoughts.
- ✓ It is a more dependable strategy for communication.
- ✓ It is effective, adaptable for all.
- ✓ It is incredible, flexible methods for persuasion and control.

Technique. No.27

Rehearsals

Before anything else, preparation is the key to success. -Alexander Graham Bell

What do you mean by reharsals ? preparation? Is this just simply reading a book? That is thoughtful, but not the best. Reading a book might be helpful, if an individual can attempts to practice thoughts with confidence, applying the concepts of the book only successfully. Without preparation and practice, we might not get fruitful results.

How much time would it be advisable for you to give to setting up your speeches? A standard thumb rule, dependable guideline is that every minute of speaking time expects one to two long hours of preparation time—maybe more, contingent upon the measure of research required for the speech. This may appear to be a ton of time; however, the rewards are definitely worth it. The legitimate preparation can decrease anxiety in front of large audiences by up to 75 percent.

Technique. No.28

Avoid Sloth (Negligence)

Luck is a result of careful preparation, failure is a result of negligence ~Robert H

Negligence in the speaker (otherwise called Sloth / lethargy) is reluctance to movement, activity or effort despite holding the ability to act or to endeavour. Laziness may be visible in the reflection an absence of confidence, self-esteem, an absence of positive acknowledgment by others, an absence of discipline. Being a speaker neglects and fails to practise the proper presentation or speech. Sloth, or sluggishness, is submitted by speakers who neglect to plan their own speech or presentation to impart to the audience. Speaking in public, regardless of whether officially or casually, that requires effort and continues practice. However, most individuals use no ambition to improve their practicality as a speaker.

To overcome this,can execute the following action plans.

- ✓ Enrol in a public speaking course
- ✓ Read public speaking books and web information
- ✓ Study incredible speakers
- ✓ Hire an expert speaking mentor

Technique. No. 29

Avoid Envy (Jealousy)

Jealousy is an inner consciousness of one's own inferiority. It is a mental cancer. - B. C. Forbes

Jealousy generally refers to the thoughts or feelings of insecurity, fear, and concern over the relative lack of possessions or safety. Jealousy can consist of one or more emotions such as anger, resentment, inadequacy, helplessness or disgust. A narrow-minded speaker will exhibit the phase of jealousy stating that incredible speakers are just fortunate to have been brought into the world with common speaking abilities.

As usual, we might have heard the reasons, like mentioned below:-

- ➢ "She's so fortunate! She's a characteristic speaker!"
- ➢ "It's so natural for him to talk before individuals."
- ➢ "No, I was unable to convey the offer. I'm not a great speaker."

Jealousy is a good indication that you are doing things the right way. People never get jealous of losers.

Technique. No.30

Avoid Lust (Sensuality)

Lust is a poor, weak, whimpering, whispering thing compared with that richness and energy of desire which will arise when lust has been killed.C. S. Lewis

"Lust is a psychological force producing intense wish for an object or circumstance." Lust can take any form such as the lust for money or power. It is distinguished from passion in that passion propels individuals to achieve benevolent goals whilst lust does not.

As public speaker lust, mentality wants their audience to praise & love them, they do not mind to criticize other speakers. In the lust speaker will be overstressed, their own abilities and raise your spirits to become a super hero, gaining respect from their audience.

"Gracefulness is a correct life: sensuality which contemplates and forms itself."— Karl Wilhelm Friedrich Schlegel

Technique. No.31

Avoid Gluttony (Excess)

Gluttony kills more than the sword – proverb

Gluttony the over indulgence and over consumption of anything to the point of waste.

Gluttony / Excess is worse. Psychological exploration shows that individuals have a restricted ability to retain data. Over-burdening that limit will diminish their capacity to assimilate anything by any means!

Gluttony for the speaker is a situation in which he will take excess speech, slides more than they need to. Speakers who accept that more is in every case had better show excess. More slides, more shots, more models, more realities, more numbers, more subtleties, more words — a greater amount of everything.

The entirety of this greed — an excessive number of slides, such a large number of stories, such a large number of subtleties — drives the speaker down an unclear and dirty way towards.

Technique. No. 32

Greed (Self-indulgence)

Greed is the lack of confidence of one's own ability to create.
Greed is a bottomless pit, which exhausts the person in an endless effort to satisfy the need without ever reaching satisfaction. Erich Fromm

Greed' signifies a strong, egotistical and selfish desire for something. People who are greedy can never be happy or satisfied in their life since greed can never be satisfied. It is something which has no limit.

In terms of public speaker, speaking for more than your assigned time misuses the promise you have with your audience, and that is rarely acceptable. Individuals are occupied and do not value having their time squandered. No one will complaint in the event that you finish a couple of moments early. On the off chance that you go over the long time hours together, negative feelings start to occupy the room, making you more powerless. Greediness is the deadly sin of overabundance, and is submitted by a speaker who goes over the long run.

Technique. No. 33

Avoid Wrath (Anger)

Anger doesn't solve anything it builds nothing, but it can destroy everything.

Wrath indicates strong merciless anger or outrage. Wrath is great anger that expresses itself in a wish to punish someone. Wrath is also used symbolically of things that behave in a violent way. It is an intense emotional state involving a strong uncomfortable and non-cooperative response to a perceived provocation, hurt, or threat.

A speaker who handles issues in the absolute worst manner submits uncontrolled displeasure. As a speaker, you ought to consistently stay motivated. Regardless of how terrible the speaker presentation is going, try to avoid panicking.

- When you commit an error (even a major one), cope-up telling more example.
- When an audience part is disturbing the room, "settle" it with mockery.
- When the room or scene coordination fizzle, do not begin accusing the coordinators or any other individual.
- When an audience part is bothering you, do not take the trap.

Technique. No.34

Avoid Arrogance

There are two kinds of pride, both good and bad. 'Good pride' represents our dignity and self-respect. 'Bad pride' is the deadly sin of superiority that reeks of conceit and arrogance. - John C. Maxwell

A speaker who accepts that public speaking is about them submits Pride. It is definitely not.

- It is never about you.
- It is never about your amazing awards in your presentation.

Public speaking is consistently about the audience and the message you need to pass on. Neglecting to put the audience first will slaughter any presentation. Public speaking is consistently about the audience and the message you need to pass on."

Arrogance is a creature. It does not have senses. It has only a sharp tongue and the pointing finger. - Toba Beta

Technique. No. 35

Story telling

The most powerful person in the world is the storyteller. The storyteller sets the vision, values and agenda of an entire generation that is to come. - Steve Jobs

Telling a story on a stage will help the speaker to overcome the stage fear. Stories that identify with your theme are another approach to keep grown-ups intrigued by your presentation. Utilized selectively inside your presentation, these stories not just make interest; they often help to loosen you up too. Storytelling creates an Immersive Experience

- Storytelling Inspires Audiences to Take Action
- People tend to be driven by their feelings.
- Hence, utilizing a solid story to take advantage of the feelings of your crowd is an extraordinary method for convincing activity.
- Storytelling makes your Presentation more memorable.

Story telling is the most powerful way to put ideas into the world today - Robert Mckee

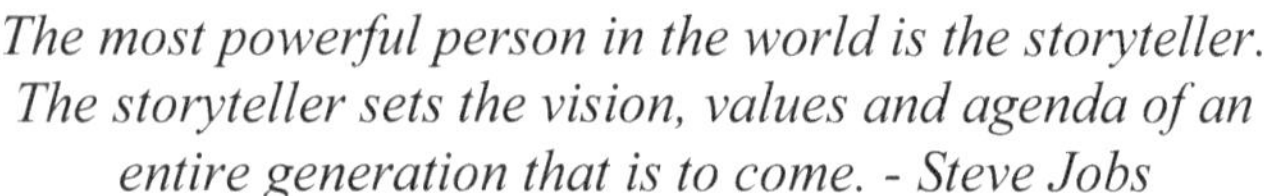

Technique. No. 36

Change your negative talk

None can destroy iron, but its own rust can. Likewise, none can destroy a person but its own mindset can. ~ Ratan Tata

We invest much of our time expressing self-criticism, smart enough, revealing to ourselves that we are not sufficient, keen enough, skilled enough, talented or adequately slight. Our negative self-talk influences us in an incredible manner on the off chance that we believe it is unthinkable, we will not try to attempt it.

SOS Negative self-talk stopping technique

Stop - Mentally tell yourself "Stop" to give you the opportunity to address the thought and interrupt the cycle.

Observe: Observe what you are saying to yourself and how it is making you feel

Shift: Shift your cognitive, emotional or behavioural response by using positive coping skills and techniques

At the point when you experience the impacts of negative thoughts contemplations –, for example, considerations that make the enthusiastic conditions of dread, fear, nervous, anxiety, shy, outrage, uneasiness, blame, disgrace, or lament:

- ✓ The muscles in your body really become more vulnerable or weaker.
- ✓ Your nervousness or stress levels go up.
- ✓ And How to Overcome Them
- ✓ Never think continuously negative thinking

You need to understand that despite the fact that stage fright is "all in the brain," the fear shows itself genuinely.

Technique. No. 37

Don't run for perfection

"People call me a perfectionist, but I'm not. I am a rightist. I do something until its right, and then I move on to the next thing."— *James Cameron*

As you work on your speeches, ensure you prepare altogether and do everything you can to make yourself clear to your audience members. Nevertheless, do not freeze about being perfect or about what will occur in the event that you commit an error. Once you free your brain of these weights, you will think that it is a lot simpler to approach your speeches with certainty and even with energy and enthusiasm

- Your Progress is more important than perfection. Focus on progress, not perfection
- Trying to be perfect can get in the way of healthy changes you are trying to make.
- Learn how focusing on first progress, then perfection
- Look for the Value of your Goals Strive for excellence but with a passion

Perfection hinders new ideas and ways of doing things. It might likewise assist with realizing that there is nothing of the sort as a perfect speech. By Amy M. Charland

Checklist for the Progress to avoid stage fear

Sl.No	Checklist	Yes	No
1	Enthusiastic about speech topic?		
2	Thoroughly developed the content of my speech?		
3	Introduction so my speech will get off to a good start?		
4	Have I worked on the conclusion so my speech will end on a strong note?		
5	Have I rehearsed my speech orally until I am confident about its delivery?		
6	Have I worked on turning negative thoughts about my speech into positive ones?		
7	Do I realize that nervousness is normal, even among experienced speakers?		
8	Do I understand that most nervousness is not visible to the audience?		
9	Am I focused on communicating with my audience, rather than on worrying about my nerves?		
10	Have I visualized myself speaking confidently and getting a positive response from the audience ?		

Technique. No. 38

Gain public speaking experience

If you can speak, you can influence. If you can influence, you can change lives

Recall your first day at kindergarten, your first day at a new position. You were presumably anxious in every situation since you were confronting something new and obscure. When you are acquainted with the situation, it was done undermining. Therefore, it is with public speaking. For most research, the greatest piece of anxiety in front of large audiences is dread of the obscure. The more you find out about public speaking and the more speeches you give, the less compromising speechmaking will turn into.

Gaining public speaking will helps you plan appropriately, engage with the audience, cope with nerves, and watch recordings of your speeches. Carefully articulate and pronounce your words. Avoid filler words. Words such as "um," "ah," "you know," Obviously, the way to self-confidence may have sometimes up and downs. It continues by experimentation or trial and error. A positive thought process of psychological physical will help to generate energy to a speaker for his speech.

Technique. No.39

Avoid un-avoidable disturbance on your stage performance

Things do not disturb people, but by the view, they take of them. ~ Epictetus

More often, speaker recognize noisy disturbance or interruption. This should be possible to deal in a gentle & humorous manner. This permits your audience to show a response to the noise and they refocus their consideration regarding you and your show.

If by chance, the audience may be unacknowledged, but definitely later most of the audience will realize the disturbance. Considering what the noise was or how much harm was done. It is advisable to hold or pause the presentation for a few seconds, and later you proceed with your stage show.

Technique. No.40

Gestures & words of speech both should match

Speech is power; speech is to persuade, to convert, to compete - Ralph wild Emerson

What happens when the words you communicate in and your body language do not coordinate or do not match? Audiences will eventually accept body language all the time. Our minds are normally developed to unconscious reading of others' body language.

Therefore, our oblivious unconscious minds are truly reading the intent of  individuals by what they sees. At the point when individuals address us, we unwittingly look and compare their words and body language. At the point when they are not adjusted, we will accept the body language as opposed to the words verbally expressed. Overall, when we are doing business, the audience can perceive what you are not saying. Therefore, if your body language does not coordinate or match your words, then, it is not fruitful transaction.

Technique. No.41

Simplify & stay on message

"If you can't explain it simply, you don't understand it well enough." - Albert Einstein

Making your speech in a simple manner will help to overcome the stage fear. Let us take this self-explanatory example: "Numbers and figures. Love them or disdain them, they can give the results, outcomes and proof your presentation needs to represent a point. Keeping it simple does not mean dead presentation, but adhere to the systematic techniques as mentioned below

- Utilize simple, direct language, no complicated terms. Know your subject!
- Audience Driven Methodology -"How will an audience see my work?"
- Clear Substance Procedure -Before you start composing your presentation, think about building your substance around a subject
- Make Numbers Significant, meaningful or self-explanatory.
- Know the point you need to make!
- Know your design and structure of speech
- Realize your audience well
- Provide testimonials and case studies
- Picture a person when you are communicating Make it readable.

Technique. No.42

Punctuate words with signals

You can speak well if your tongue can deliver the message of your heart - John Ford

Gestures should supplement your words in amicability. Disclose to them how large the fish was and show them with your arms. A punctuation mark is an imprint, or sign, utilized in writing and speaking into expressions and sentences to make meaning clear.

- Utilization of the wrong characteristic of punctuation or even the wrong arrangement of the sign of punctuation can change the importance of the sentence totally and here and there even believe the sentence to finish garbage.
- Utilizing punctuation in your writing assists the reader or speaker with plainly understanding the message that is being conveyed.
- A wrongly utilized punctuation or missing punctuation can change the whole importance & meaning of a sentence.

- Punctuation fundamentally assists with demonstrating the pauses and the emphasis on certain ideas or thoughts that are discussed in the text.
- Especially, in writing or speeches it is essential to accurately use punctuation as it helps to strengthen arguments that are made in the text.

Technique. No.43

Envision the outcome

Communication works for those who work at it.
John Powel

Call it what you will: reflection, perception, contemplation. Whatever you call it, get it done. Invest energy picturing yourself giving an ideal introduction and speaking in public – loaded up with humour, warmth, certainty and knowledge.

Technique. No.44

Practice, Practice, Practice

There is no glory in Practice, but without practice, there is No glory

Practice is one of the major tools to avoid the stage fear. Practice Changes the Brain in Unique Ways Research indicates short periods of practice can actually enhance the brain's plasticity and change its structure. You need to practice, however, as much as you can before the presentation or public speaking.

Practice or Rehearsal is important because you can apply your knowledge of public speaking to test out what works for you and learn from the experience in a safe environment. It allows you to practice different parts before you actually deliver the total speech to an audience.

- Structured Practice Is Efficient
- The better you manage your practice session time, the faster you will learn in an organised manner.
- Practice Helps Internalize
- Practice Inculcates Discipline

Practice makes perfect. After a long time of practicing, our work will become natural, skilful, swift, and stead. - Bruse Lee

Technique. No. 45

Avoid Jargons

Aim for brevity while avoiding Jargon. ~ Edsger Dijkstra

Using more jargons makes the speaker psychologically uncomfortable or confused. Let us ask question for self why should you avoid jargon? What you are trying to accomplish. Do you want to communicate a new idea to clients and customers, or are you demonstrating your expertise to colleagues in the field?

Whatever your decision, make sure that your writing creates understanding in your audience, not confusion.

- Use simple words and phrases.
- Avoid hidden verbs.
- Avoid noun strings.
- Avoid jargon.
- Minimize abbreviations.
- Minimize definitions.
- Use the same terms consistently.
- Place words carefully.

Technique. No.46

Remember to make open gestures

Simple, little gestures change the world for the better.

To ignore stage fear symptoms, ensure your gestures are extensively visible to the audience in a broader way.

- Hand Moments
- Walk on the stage
- Have a positive posture
- Keep your head up.
- Avoid Uncrossed Legs & Arms

Technique. No.47

Getting through the first 5 Minutes

The lost time is never found again. ~ Benjamin Franklin

The whole introduction is just five minutes in length. This will make it less distressing. Zero in on traversing the initial five minutes, and at this point you will just quiet down and the rest is downhill.

Technique. No.48

Don't shiver your legs on stage

Effective communication depends much more on your tone of voice and body language than the words you say. ~ Dalton Singh Khalsa

To avoid stage fear, do not shake your legs on stage while addressing the audience. Be studying and have flexible momentum on the stage.

Technique. No.49

Lead a conversation

A conversation is so much more than words, a conversation is eyes, smiles, the silences between the words~Annika Thor

Again, only one out of every odd speaking chance manages the cost of time for a conversation, yet realizes how to connect with the audience profitably.

One good conversation can shift the Technique of change forever - Linda Lambert.

Technique. No.50

Keep your hands out of your pockets

Take your hands out of your pocket, because life may push you hardly at any time

To be confident and avoid stage fear, keep your hands out of your pockets.

Body language is the scope of nonverbal signs that you used to convey your emotions and aims. These incorporate your posture, facial expression and hand gestures.

Your capacity to comprehend and interpret body language can assist you to come up from the stage fear. You can likewise utilize body language in a positive manner to add solidarity to your verbal messages.

Technique. No.51

It isn't all about you

If you have no confidence in self, you are twice defeated in the race of life. ~ Marcus.G

In spite of the fact that you may feel like everybody is out to giggle, reprimand or judge you, which is not the situation. Get over the inclination that the world will hold all your mix-ups.Zero in on your discourse, audience and what they merit from you. This will facilitate the pressing factor that is now gathering.

Technique. No. 52

Stop unwanted signalling

Experience tells you what to do, Confidence allows you to do it. ~ Stan Smith

Avoid unnecessary signalling to your team members. Please practise your coordination issues before the speaker enters the stage. Nervousness on stage is common, we must handle it gentle.

Technique. No.53

Keep moving while you talk

Do not give. Great things take time

Maybe you can recount a narrative story that identifies with your subject and moves around as you advise it. There is something brilliant about a presenter who moves around as he or she talks.

Technique. No.54

Twice check everything

When you doubt your power, you give power to your doubt.

Do you have a Personal Computer or any audio video notes? Watch that everything works. At the point when you stroll in front of an audience and out of nowhere, understand that you failed to remember your notes; it is past the point of no return. Obviously, your nerves will dominate. Know your discourse or introduction so well that should this occur, you can proceed effortlessly.

Technique. No.55

Use body signs & gestures in-between chest & Waist

Always be yourself; express yourself have faith in yourself. Do not go out, look for a successful personality, and duplicate ~ Bruce lee

While speaking, presenting, introducing in professional (Formal) meetings, attempt to keep your gestures between chest & waist level for the vast majority of the presentation. Utilize the chest or headspaces of the body for focus and to make focuses stick. It exhibits more confidence.

The gestures below survey reveals "seemed a bit closed off and slightly uncomfortable." Low gestures normally makes us lower our energy and read as less confident

Technique. No.56

Have a secondary thought, at the point when things turn out badly

Failing to plan is planning to fail. Allen Lakein

Sometimes, something will turn out badly. Your projector or amplifier may quit working. On the off chance that you definitely realize your substance, at that point chances are that this will not upset you so much. On the off chance that, for example, your amplifier quits working, do not worry about it, continue with a stronger voice. Odds are the specialized individuals are as of now pushing and attempting to figure the issue out, so you being stressed over a similar issue will not ashelp.

Productivity is never an accident. It is always the result of a commitment to excellence, intelligent planning, and focused effort. ~ Paul J Meyer

Technique. No.57

Use different types of media

If you want to chase the success, you have to let the time chase you

A presentation can quickly become boring and monotonous. To avoid this, it is advisable to use different types of media. For example, combine videos and flipcharts use the whiteboard or show something practical on a model. This will increase the attention of your audience enormously and will help in keeping them engaged until the end.

Technique. No.58

Ignore subconscious physical habits

Bad habits are like chains that are too light to feel until they are too heavy to carry. Warren Buffet

Ignore subconscious Physical relaxation habits like

- Yawning not closing your face with hands.
- Popping or Cracking your bubble Gum
- Making intentional fun on the audience Misfortunes
- Playing with your hair
- Doing weird things with your hands

Technique No.59

Use a laser pointer

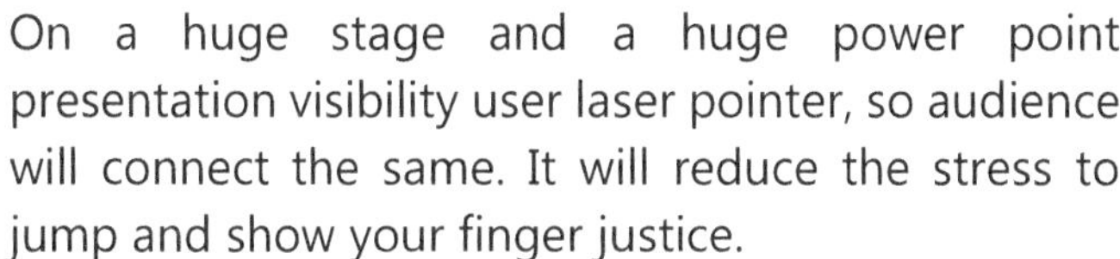

On a huge stage and a huge power point presentation visibility user laser pointer, so audience will connect the same. It will reduce the stress to jump and show your finger justice.

Technique No.60

Step by step explanation

To avoid fear gestures on stage, start your speech slowly and explain systematically to get confidence.

Technique No.61

Emotional Intelligence

To overcome use some sentiment words so the audience will connect, and as a speaker, you will be comfortable on stage.

Technique No.62

Interact with the audience, that makes you more comfortable before you make speech

Ask questions (and care about the appropriate responses). Request volunteers. Make your presentation an exchange.

Technique No.63

Focus

Help your audience handle your message by zeroing in on your message. Stories, humour, or other "sidebars" ought to be associated with the centre of thought. Anything that does not should be altered out.

Technique No.64

Obey time imperatives

In any case, redo your presentation to fit the time permitted, and regard your audience by not going over the long run.

Technique No.65

Expertise a presentation

Set the unique circumstance and ensure the audience is all set, regardless of whether the presentation is for you or for another person.

Technique No.66

Handle startling issues easily

Maybe the power cuts, the lights will go out. Perhaps the projector is dead. Have an arrangement to deal with each situation.

Technique No.67

Be cognizant when speaking spur of the moment

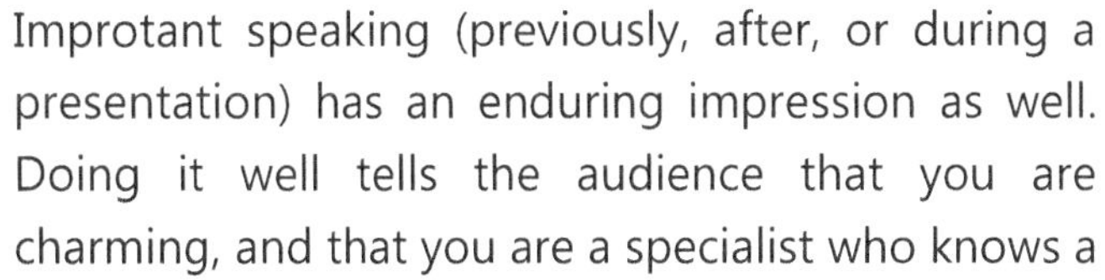

Improtant speaking (previously, after, or during a presentation) has an enduring impression as well. Doing it well tells the audience that you are charming, and that you are a specialist who knows a great deal past the slides and arranged speech.

Technique No.68

Seek and use criticism

Understand that no presentation or presenter (indeed, even you!) is great. Focus on nonstop improvement, and comprehend that the ideal approach to improve is to request authentic input from however, many individuals as you can.

Technique No.69

Organize thoughts legitimately

An efficient presentation can be caught up with insignificant mental strain. Spanning is critical.

Technique No.70

Use quotes, realities, and measurements

During the presentation on stage, we might forget the subject points, if you remember and use the quotations and real instances; this will be fuel for your speech. Use it fittingly to supplement your thoughts.

Technique No.71

Make pauses during speech

Taking a break can lead to breakthroughs. ~ Russell Eric Dobda

To avoid the stage fear and to become an effective public speaker, use the appropriate pause techniques. It will help the speaker in the following manner

- Pauses indicate a change in tone or topic
- It emphasizes key points
- Grab attention
- Regain control-recall what you want to say
- Make sentences clear
- Understanding
- Emphasis what you want to say
- Transition for both the speaker & the audience
- Replace a filler in a or a hesitation word
- Let the applause finish
- Think of a response to a question

Technique No.72

Start introduction strong and close stronger

The right word may be effective, but no word was ever as effective as a rightly timed pause Mark Twain

The body of your presentation ought to be solid as well; however, your audience will recall your first and final words (assuming, in reality,recollect that anything by any means).

To ignore the nervousness and stress on stage, the speaker should ensure that the appropriate gentle smile should shown to the audience.

Technique No.73

Music

Where words fail, music speaks. ~ Hans Christian Andersen

Music will help the speaker to overcome the stage fear, diverting nervousness to relaxation. Music can also stimulate the mind. There are many things in music to which one can listen and bring attention.  Music can raise someone's mood, get him or her excited, or make them calm and relaxed. Music also - and this is important - allows us to feel nearly or possibly all emotions that we experience in our lives.

- Universal language
- Create a good ambiance
- Emotions
- Music makes education more enjoyable
- Music can create a mood
- Bind people together
- Evoke strong emotions
- Music induced trance
- A confidence booster for you
- Filler during your presentation
- Music imagery and hallucinations

Technique No.74

Speak loud & clear.

Your message is only as loud as the actions that accompany it. Live your message and it will be heard loud and clear. - Rev kellen Roggenbuck

Do not talk in a quiet, modest manner. You are making a presentation to a large group of audience. Projecting your voice loud and clear is the way to overcome your fears of public speaking as well. Staying quiet and shy increases anxiety while speaking louder than usual naturally forces you to exude confidence.

- Kindly remember, as a speaker you are going to address a group of audience in an auditorium, meeting room, class or anywhere: Project Your Voice Loud and Clear.
- Your voice can send out your message to the world
- Our voices can connect to, inspire, and change those around us
- Both clear and loud speech show promise for improving intelligibility and maintaining or improving speech severity in multitasker babble for speakers
- When speaking in a loud voice, it is easy to end in a lower pitch, which sounds confident.

Technique No.75

Take on schedule interval or break

Sometimes when we take a break, we may find that solutions then present themselves. ~Catherine Pulsifer

Please remember, even a speaker or audience are a human being, it's necessary to take the breaks. If there are no breaks, the speaker will be under nervousness to complete his presentation. This break or interval will help the trainer to prepare the next subject.

It Improves memory. It has been shown that short, repeated sessions of learning with breaks increase your concentration and facilitate the memorization of new content. A few advantages are mentioned below

- Serves as energy boosts
- Reduces stress
- Improves your health
- Boosts your performance and creativity.

Technique No.76

Play videos

No technology is better at conveying emotion than video.

Video is more persuasive than other types of content because the human brain requires emotional input to make decisions. No technology is better at conveying emotion than video. This is because video caters to both the brains' visual and auditory systems and it will influence a person's choices or action.

A new infographic from Wyzowl shows that only 10% of people remember what they hear. Reading does not help much either since only about 20% of people remember what they read. Conversely, 80% of people remember what they see and do. In addition, it is more than just that. They also learned that visuals are processed 60,000x faster than text and that 93% of communication is nonverbal.

- Visual stimulation grabs students' attention
- Video emphasizes digital literacy
- The stimulation of higher-order learning
- Videos are excellent marketing tools

Technique No.77

Dress-up properly.

It reflects a good character. Dressing well and staying well-groomed conveys more than just power, authority, and confidence.

Dressing up is an opportunity to be creative, make a good impression, boost your confidence, and purposefully present yourself to the world.

- It leaves a great impression
- It makes you believe in yourself
- It attracts the right crowd
- It keeps productivity flowing
- It reflects a good character

- Dressing well helps the audience to pay attention to you
- It is a form of self-care
- It helps to lead the competitive edge
- Dressing well helps to build consistency
- Dressing well keeps you disciplined
- It can bring joy into other people's lives
- It increases your confidence
- Dressing well gives you a feeling of accomplishment
- Dressing well makes you look and feel good!
- First impressions count.

Technique No.78

Learn from past failures

Do not waste time grieving over past mistakes, learn from them and move on.

Learning from the past failures or overcomes of the earlier presentation will help you to become an effective public speaker, and it brings confidence to you and you may over come stage fear.

- It helps to redefine your priorities in life
- It makes you more compassionate
- You look to your faith in a higher power

Technique No.79

Stick to your theme only

Show your unique charisma, be yourself.

Stick to a certain topic, Keep content clear and brief. Schedule your speech at a time when people are likely to be most engaged.

- Ask questions or perform actions that keep the audience involved and invested.
- Consider language and rhetoric.
- Appeal to the emotions of the audience.
- End with a memorable moment.

Technique No.80

Let Some Questions Go

Knowledge is having the right answer. Intelligence is asking the right question

A presentation is a shared experience between the presenter and members of the audience. In asking questions, the speaker should ask questions to all students in the classroom. Questions shall be given to all the participants to encourage them to participate in the teaching and learning process
The questions should contain the following concepts

- Knowledge
- Understanding
- Application
- Analysis
- Combination
- Evaluation

"Successful people ask better questions, and as a result, they get better answers." ~ Anthony Robbins

Technique No.81

Don't compare yourself with others

Do not compare your life to others. There is no comparison between the sun and the moon, they shine when it is their time Some flowers grow best in the sun and some grow well in the shade. Remember god puts us where we can grow best, so always be a happy in every situation of life.

- It is you vs you. Compare yourself with you.
- Love your past.
- There is one thing that you are better at than other people are.
- Water your grass and invest yourself.
- Turn comparison into inspiration
- Comparing yourself to others is a recipe for unhappiness.
- Accept where you are
- You can be anything,but you cannot be everything.
- Get aware that this is not the end of the life
- Compare yourself to who you were yesterday.
- Decide not to let fear guide your choices
- You can be anything but you cannot be everything, think about your dream life.

Technique No.82

Don't Be So Hard on Yourself

Do not be too hard on yourself. There are plenty of people willing to do that for you. Love yourself and be proud of everything that you do. Even mistakes mean you are trying.

Your mistakes are part of your learning. Learn to be resilient in the face of failure. Every speaker will have his or her own merits and demerits. If you have stage fear and something went wrong, it is acceptable. It is part of your learning.

- Stand up for what you believe, even if it is unpopular. Make everyone understand your big, crazy ideas.
- Learn from people who criticize you.
- Accept your weaknesses as your "features".
- Surround yourself with people who want you to succeed.

Being hard on yourself is not only incapable, lastly, extend your definition of achievement by expanding your extent of what qualifies as a "win."

Technique No.83

Ethical Public Speaker

Efforts and courage are not enough without purpose and Technique. ~ John F Kennedy

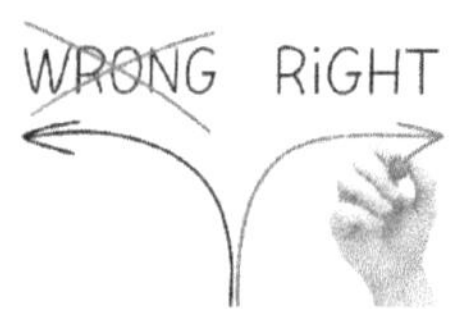

To speak ethically is to provide honest facts with integrity and without deception or distortion. To be honest, that speaker might not have all the answers. Either ethical speakers do not intentionally deceive their audience by presenting falsehoods or opinions disguised as fact; or by warping the facts to make their points. To be honest, that speaker might not have all the answers. The Qualities of an Ethical speaker are as follows

- Trustworthiness
- Integrity in the subject matter
- Respect for others
- Dignity in conduct
- Truthfulness in message
- The speech you are doing is having moral
- Use the information that is truthful
- Avoid biases and stereotypes
- Believe in your own claims
- Be prepared

Technique. No. 84

SECS Principle

Ethics knows the difference between what you have a right to do and what is right to do. ~ Potter Stewart

The SECS principle is made up of four key elements that will find it easy to become a good public speaker.

1. Sincerity,
2. Enthusiasm,
3. Confidence
4. Simplicity

It is important to choose a topic that speakers are excited by and find interesting because this will likely come across in the speech that you give, increasing the likelihood that you achieve your speech's purpose.

1. Sincerity

A speaker must be sincere if one wants to communicate with any audience – whether it is one person or one hundred. A good topic will help you be sincere. Sincerity means a number of things; it means being honest with your audience, it means you believe in what you are saying.

2. Enthusiasm

The speaker must have a genuine enthusiasm and personal interest in what it is you want to talk about, and a good topic will genuinely enthuse you.

3. Confidence

The speaker needs to be convinced that what you say is true that it is worth saying, and that it fulfils a purpose. In order to acquire this conviction, you must be confident that you know your subject. While it does not mean that you have to know everything there is to know about your subject, you should perform whatever research necessary in order to fully understand the subject for discussion.

4. Simplicity

Simplicity: keeping your presentation simple, logical and straightforward. This does not mean that your talk should be simplistic; it means that your message must be uncomplicated, unambiguous, to the point, and understandable. Choosing a good topic, one that you know about and are comfortable speaking about will help you keep it simple.

Technique No.85

Believe in yourself

Believe in yourself. You are braver than you think. More talented than you know and capable of more than you imagine.

Being a public speaker or stage performer, you must believe in yourself. It will give you self-confidence and you will overcome the stage fear.

Set Expectations and Know Your Values In Life. In business and your own life, fearlessness is essential for making a gigantic move. You need to have confidence in yourself – in your capacities, abilities and interests – to bring the jump into business or some other desire.

Believe in yourself is simply the lynchpin of excellent authority, since certainty allows you to oversee and motivate others with confirmation and heading.

Technique No.86

Conquer your limits & beliefs

You do not become what you want, you become what you believe. ~ Oprah Winfrey

Asking how to believe in yourself opens the entryway for a more profound inquiry: What are the beliefs

that are causing these feelings in any case? Negative feelings or emotions such as self-uncertainty or nervousness are profoundly associated with opinions. Every time you get a negative inner speech, change your self talk by replacing those remarks with positive contemplations.

The tips to overcome the self-limitation

- ✓ Become aware of limiting thoughts.
- ✓ Stop Doing What Others Do
- ✓ Begin to think big and see the possibilities.
- ✓ Take action toward the big dreams that confront the limiting beliefs.
- ✓ Let your creativity blossom
- ✓ Surround yourself with other Big Dreamers.
- ✓ Continue to Grow

Technique No.87

The power of Proximity

Proximity is power. If you can get proximity with people that are the best in the world, things can happen because all of the people they know, the insights they have and the life experience they have. They can save you a decade of time by one insight. - Tonny Robbins

Proximity is power! Whether it is your business, health, finances, or relationships – surrounding yourself with people who are already successful in that area.

Learning how to believe in yourself is like running a race set on an uphill course. You will need fuel for the journey. To fuel self-belief, surround yourself with people who inspire and support you. This is the law of attraction – the idea that, as Tony says, "Proximity is power." Whatever you want to achieve in your life, find people who will elevate you, not bring you down.

The simple act of whom you spend your time with is who you become. In other words, surround yourself with people who have already achieved your goals, people who you admire and people who are playing the game at a higher level than you are.

Technique No.88

Nourish your Mind

Fill your brain with giant dreams, so there is no room for Petty purists. ~ Robbin Sharma

Being a trainer or a public speaker, it is very important to have continuous improvement and continuous learning. This will make the speaker be confident on the stage, the same he will perform well. The law of attraction is not just about who you associate with. It's also, about how you feed your mind. Watch documentaries about people who have done great things in life. Read inspirational quotes and write down your favourites. Learn about new topics that will help you reach your goals, it will help you face your fears – like how to be confident or deliver a presentation.

The advantages of nourishing the mind tips

- ✓ Create the right environment
- ✓ Increased Immunity
- ✓ Focus on one task at a time
- ✓ Improve wellness
- ✓ Eat "smart" foods
- ✓ Spend time in nature
- ✓ Meditate
- ✓ Be positive with yourself

Technique No.89

Focus Change

Instead of obsessing over the things you cannot change, focus on what you can your attitude, your mind set, your energy ~ Mandy Hale

The stage performer should always self-motivated. This is one of the best practices to overcome stage

fright. This can be possible to have an optimal focus of the performer. Some of the time, you do not have to look for help from outside sources to put stock in yourself. In case you are feeling weak, in some cases, you should simply move your focus.

Rather than focusing on disappointments or shortcomings, recall minutes in your past in which you were fruitful at a comparative assignment or in which your qualities radiated through.

Advantages of Focus Change

Personal growth   Strength
Flexibility   Progress
Improvements   Opportunities
Life values   New beginnings

Technique No.90

Face your Fears

Fight your fears and you will be in a battle forever. Face your fears and you will be free forever. ~ Lucas Jonkman

It is a human instinct to encounter fear and anxiety. In any case, when you trust in yourself, you understand that those emotions are there to urge you to make a move, not to keep you down.

"Fear doesn't shut you down; it wakes you up."— Veronica Roth

Face your fears by making objectives that are associated with your general reason throughout everyday life. Laying out and accomplishing objectives that assist you with beating, your fears will give you a feeling of achievement.

Fear conquering truths

FEAR: False **E**vidence **A**ppearing **R**eal

- ✓ It's okay to be afraid
- ✓ It's best to start taking actions to face fear
- ✓ Do what you are afraid of
- ✓ Everybody feels fear
- ✓ Your personal growth can only happen when you face your fear

Fight your fears and doubts, and new worlds will open to you.

Technique No.91

Develop a Growth Mind-set

Mistakes are PROOF you are TRYING, Correcting mistakes are PROOF that you are GROWING
- James Anderson

A growth mindset means one embraces challenges, persists in the face of setbacks, takes responsibility for their words and actions, and acknowledges that effort is the path toward mastery. It is the reason why "practice makes perfect."

Tips to develop a growth mind-set

- ✓ Face your challenges bravely.
- ✓ Pay attention to your words and thoughts
- ✓ Cultivate a sense of purpose
- ✓ Turn criticism around until you find its gift
- ✓ Learn from the mistakes of others
- ✓ Direction is more important than speed
- ✓ Great works are performed, not by strength, but by perseverance.
- ✓ It takes courage to grow up and become who you really are.

Technique No.92

Continuous learning new Skills

I can accept failure, everyone fails at something.
But I can't accept not trying - Michael Jordan

Research has proven that learning is related to happiness – it releases dopamine in the brain, known as the "reward molecule." By continuing to learn, the speaker or stage performer can more easily step out their comfort zone and take on new opportunities.

- ✓ Remain relevant. Don't be left behind
- ✓ Prepare for the unexpected
- ✓ Boost your profile
- ✓ Competence leads to confidence
- ✓ Sparks new ideas
- ✓ Change your perspective
- ✓ Pay it forward

One way to begin to develop a growth mindset is to challenge yourself to learn new things. Continuous learning a new skill can increase your feelings of self-efficacy – your belief in your abilities to execute tasks, control your own behaviour and attain your goals.

Technique No.93

Focus your Inner Strengths

Strength does not come from physical capacity. It comes from an indomitable will. ~ Mahatma Gandhi

Why is it important to believe in yourself? Self-belief is about finding your inner strength so that you can embrace the journey that is life, with all its difficulties, and realize that each challenge brings new skills, understanding and strength.

- ✓ We all have times when we just do not think we can do it. The most important thing is to never give up.
- ✓ You will inevitably encounter obstacles, but it is how you react to them that matters.
- ✓ Believing in yourself is all about digging deep and realigning your focus on what you really want in life: discovering how to believe in yourself. It truly is within your reach.

Technique No.94

Be Equal & Favourite to all

Giving the equal opportunities with all your audience will be more favourable to all the audience. This is one of method to overcome the stage fear.

Technique No.95

Break up your Presentation

If you want to overcome from the stage fear, kindly make your presentation on chapter wise or priority wise. These kind of breakups in the speech will helpful to the speaker.

Technique No.96

Remember you cannot satisfy all the audience, remove unnecessary nervousness with in you

Kindly remember not all five fingers are in equal size, the same way the audience are differ from with others. Do your best to get the Best result?

Technique No.97

Engage the Audience

Engaging actively with the audience will help you to mingle with them, and you can avoid your stage fear.

Technique No.98

Explain. Don't read your presentation

An effective Public Speaker will follow the principle to interact, explain the presentation to the audience. This will boost the willpower of the speaker and overcome the stage fear. In your speech kindly, do not read your presentation, talk or explain it.

Technique No.99

Know how to start & Finish

Many will start fast, few will finish strong. GaryRyan

If you know well, how to start and how to finish with grateful thoughts, it will help you to become an effective speaker and helps you and overcome the stage fear. The following tips will help you.

- Decide to finish
- Make a plan
- commit to the task
- Start
- Make your deadline
- Track your progress
- Don't just finish it, complete it
- Celebrate what you have done

Technique No.100

Focus on the camera & audience

Being a public speaker or stage performer, the objective is to reach the audience and program record. For this, as speaker should be focused on the camera and audience frequently. This confident practice will help you to avoid stage fright.

Technique No.101

Other general techniques

1. Arrive early not to be late to the event.
2. Adjust your surroundings.
3. Use simple, straightforward language.
4. Get to your subject point quickly.
5. Give self-examples or common examples that everyone comes across.
6. Preplan your event and point your date & your latest events plan.
7. Use bullet points or numbered lists.

With you and for you

Dr.Y.Narasimha Raja
Email : ynr.phd@gmail.com
Whatsapp : 09686845718

www.ingramcontent.com/pod-product-compliance
Lightning Source LLC
Chambersburg PA
CBHW071522150726
48000CB00002B/645